GRUAU

© 2004 Assouline Publishing for the present edition
601 West 26th Street, 18th floor
New York, NY 10001, USA
Tel.: 212 989-6810   Fax: 212 647-0005
www.assouline.com

First published by Assouline, Paris, France

Translated from the French by Uniontrad

Printed by Grafiche Milani (Italy)

ISBN: 2 84323 415 8

GRUAU

FRANÇOIS BAUDOT

ASSOULINE

g ruau is first of all a signature. Five black letters stroked with the tip of a paintbrush. A sign, like an onomatopoeia with a quick, sharp sound. Like the "ho!" of surprise suggested in the wake of the woman dressed by Christian Dior, and painted by René Gruau.

An entire era of elegance found an advocate in this artist, the last of a long line of Parisian poster designers: Cappiello, Forain, Cassandre, Paul Colin, etc. The nostalgia ends here, because at the ripe young age of 87, Gruau continues to draw, content to make the minute variations that allow him to remain the same as he was when he came to Paris more than half a century ago.

The history of illustration and fashion drawings developed parallel to the history of painting throughout the nineteenth century. It is difficult to separate it from the evolution of the press – especially women's magazines – and the exponential development of luxury advertising. Such images have long required the talent of great illustrators (even Jean Cocteau and Christian Bérard played their part):

the art of a sketch drawn with chic – the combination of a few strokes, a few colors, and elegant typography. If not for the nostalgia that permeates our contemporaries, those silhouettes would now be considered deliciously outdated. Yet this very nostalgia leads them to constantly reassess this heritage which, though light, conveys a grace that today often seems to be a lost secret.

An illustrator requires a great talent for observing things, speed of execution, humor, and more importantly, the ability to synthesize a situation in order to capture – in addition to the model – an attitude, the crinkling of taffeta, the softness of fur, the brittleness of a cape, or the delicious circumflex accent of a lovely bonnet balanced on a pretty head. A sketch has to have personality and originality. But it also has to sum up the spirit of the moment, to inform as tangibly as possible the eyes of those who in turn will project themselves onto those imaginary shores. There are so many ways to recreate "the period, the fashion, the moral, the passion." Baudelaire summarized this when he said that an illustrator "extracts the eternal from the transient."

Like Mallarmé – who in 1874 launched *La Dernière Mode*, a magazine he financed and wrote practically by himself – Daumier, Degas, Bonnard, Vallotton, Helleu, Boldini and many other great modern artists took an interest in clothing and accessories, much as Clouet, Holbein, Bronzino and Gainsborough did before them. From the nineteenth through the end of the twentieth century, several painters did not hesitate to use poster form – a complete iconography on paper – to express themselves. Toulouse-Lautrec remains the most illustrious representative of this "fashion

6

through painting." The paternity of Gruau's style can be found in the assurance, dynamism and synthesized approach of the painter of the *Moulin Rouge*. Like no one before him, Toulouse-Lautrec knew how to use the black of ink in his compositions. Their fluid, virtually abstract freedom stands in sharp contrast to the structured force of the typographic characters, the Belle Époque sinuosity of the lines, the punctuation of blood-like stains seemingly dropped in flight... Everything about Lautrec naturally attracted René Gruau as he himself sought to convey the enthusiasm, audaciousness and charm of his era. Today, that capacity makes him the sole survivor of the great illustrators and poster designers, all those artists who imprinted the newspaper stands, billboards and walls of Paris with that very special quality.

born in 1909 in Rimini, René grew up on the shores of the Adriatic Sea. He was the son of Count Zavagli-Ricciardelli delle Caminate, a child spoiled by a pretty mother who took him everywhere she went. From resorts to spas, from Parisian fashion fitting rooms to Monte Carlo "tea parties", he became familiar with the world that was to become his own. He was born among the fortunate of this earth. His changing, sunny and golden existence was that of a couple he formed with his mother: the count and she separated when he was three years old. But following a change in fortune, at fourteen the young man had to find work. He was so talented in doing nothing, aside from drawing, his passion. It was this ceaseless activity that enabled him to capture effortlessly everything he saw. René Gruau was to change the course of his fate with the tip of his pencil.

The child who dreamed of becoming an architect still continues today to draw — for his pleasure — Palladian perspectives whose motionless colonnades vanish into obelisk-speckled horizons. However, fate did not make him a builder. At the beginning of the 1930s he met Vera, a fashion writer, Italian like himself. This smart woman appraised his sketches and advised him — since he needed money quickly — to specialize in fashion illustration. With his sharp eye, perpetual tan and easy ways, René took his portfolio under his arm and proceeded to make the rounds of the press houses. He won people over quite naturally — and so did his work. Especially since, with the pile of magazines Vera had lent him, our job seeker got a solid education in the art and methods of pleasing the art directors of the top journals. Little by little, he began to get work. Here again, easily: Gruau admits that he never had any worries in life. A piece of paper, a pencil, nice light and a good model were all he needed, and were enough for him to make a living. To that, one could add the Paris air, that fragrance he captures so well. The young artist talked his mother into moving to the City of Light. They both welcomed the change all the more since at that time, in Italy, the black shirts of fascism were propagating behavior that was becoming an increasing cause for concern.

●

It was in Paris, where they both worked as illustrators for newspapers such as *Marianne* and *Le Figaro*, that René Gruau met Christian Dior. Friendly, gentle, and talented in drawing and good living, this young stoutish Norman, still unknown, was also struggling — with less ease than René — to overcome the misfortunes experienced by his family. A friendship was born whose development belongs to the history of fashion. In the meantime, at the age of eighteen, the attractive Italian was earning an honorable living. Among other things, he worked on those hat shows that no longer exist – those hats which comprised a key element of the female silhouette in the 1930s and 40s.

beginning in 1935, the collaboration that René Gruau began with the prestigious magazine *Fémina* turned him into an established illustrator. *Silhouettes, Le Magazine du Figaro, Marie Claire* (a weekly at the time), created by Jean Prouvost, *L'Officiel*, etc: all those magazines opened their pages to Gruau, whose drawings could be found side by side with such talented artists as Tom Keogh, Marcel Vertès, Cecil Beaton, Christian Bérard and René Willaumez, a young Breton count who had entered the world of fashion and whose influence was to be considerable. The great Carl Erikson (Eric) also collaborated with French *Vogue*, the rival of *Fémina*. Through thirty years of faithful collaboration, this artist produced true fireworks – each figurine was more masterful than the next. But the only influences that Gruau recognizes aside from Lautrec are Cappiello, the elegant poster artist of his childhood years, famous for his black backgrounds, and René Driant, a costume designer, stage set designer and painter whose talent is not sufficiently recognized today. Gruau was also influenced by the Japanese print masters and their ingenious page layouts, with their dark solid tints drawn with a skillful brush dipped in China ink. We should also mention the great illustrators of 1900s' women: Paul Helleu, Boldini, Mary Cassatt, and earlier on, the subtle illustrator Antoine Watteau, a major artist whose elegant parties provided a certain lightness compared to most of the paintings produced at the height of the baroque era.

In 1939, after the fighting, the Germans occupied the northern zone of France. The main French newspapers and the world of fashion emigrated south to the Riviera, where companies such as Worth, Hermès, and Lanvin had branches. René Gruau was quite happy to follow this movement towards the Mediterranean: for him, more than a refuge, the Côte d'Azur was a frame of mind. In Cannes, where he stayed so many times at the Carlton, he still owns an elegant apartment whose terraces open on one side onto the last ridges of the Alps, and on the other onto the moving blue ridges of the waves. Most of the time, he lives and continues to work in this peaceful environment.

t he German occupation was a period of hibernation, a heavy drama completely contrary to Gruau's carefree spirit. Moreover, while he was extremely well received by New York, the illustrator did not like America enough to want to live there. By the time France was liberated, the esteem for his art that had built up during the 1930s allowed him to embark on the third stage of his career. In the early 1950s, he was at the apex of his career. Paris was once again a party after Christian Dior triumphantly launched his new look in 1947. Almost automatically, Dior's accomplice from the early days became his official painter in his relentless march to build what has become the Dior empire of fashion, perfume, licensing and multiple luxury products. From that point on, the name René Gruau was forever associated with the name of the great couturier. For each of Dior's products, Gruau created strong visuals that appeared in both luxury magazines and on the walls of every capital in the world. Who can forget the 1948 drawing for *Eau Sauvage* (the first real toilet water for men) representing a woman's hand delicately laid on the furry paw of a large feline? Such drawings, it is said, speak more than a thousand words. In this specific case, everything was said, or inferred, to overcome the masculine reticence of talking about scents. While fashion sketches may have been a resource for the young Gruau, advertising represented the true vocation of the mature Gruau. More than the beauty and elegance of his work, or the esthetics of his black and white sketches dotted with color, each illustration contains an idea, an impact, a visual power that works every time. All the way to the 1970s, he created a series of visuals for all the Dior perfumes, from *Miss Dior* (1947) to *Dior Dior* (1978). But the artist found other objects to serve his talent: the very famous advertisement of *Rouge Baiser*, that "allows you to kiss," *Scandale* stockings or the *Jolie Madame* perfume by Pierre Balmain (1952), the Perrin and Crescendo gloves, the Montézin hats, the first perfume by Jacques Griffe (1949), and the products by Payot, Elizabeth Arden, Jantzen, Van Cleef & Arpels and others. Not to mention the *Lido*, a music hall that was very much the fad until the 1960s, for which Gruau designed monumental posters that dazzled Parisians and foreigners who recognized the perfectly idealized version of the most beautiful women of the City of Light.

•

In 1948, Gruau, who had already worked for *Harper's Bazaar*, the best American magazine at the time, moved to Manhattan. He collaborated with the legendary though short-lived magazine *Flair*. Created by Fleur Cowles and financed by her husband, the owner of *Look*, only fourteen issues of the luxurious publication were to be printed. Still, it allowed the discovery of an incredible number of talents from all lands. René Gruau was offered a contract by the wife of producer Louis B. Mayer to design the costumes for Metro-Goldwyn-Mayer. While very attractive, the proposal would have required the artist to move to Hollywood. Uncomfortable with the Beverly Hills lifestyle, Gruau could not get himself to leave France. Perhaps this is a pity. One of his predecessors, Paul Iribe, was very productive in the years he worked for the major studios, creating the sets and costumes for the Cecil B. De Mille productions. A film such as *Les Girls*, directed by George Cukor, for which Hoyningen-Huene was the artistic advisor, or *My Fair Lady* by the same director, for which the sets and costumes were designed by Cecil Beaton, are examples of the level of sophistication and talent that Gruau also could have contributed to during the Golden Age of American comedy.

already settled into his comfortable "last of the Mohicans" persona, Gruau reached his sixtieth birthday without losing an ounce of that freshness and ease he exhibited in his greatest masterpieces. However, he would sometimes repeatedly rework a drawing, being highly exacting in his judgment of each line. Each sketch generally required the presence of a posing model. Gruau drew from life: first fanciful sketches, then cropping sketches, then grouping, and then making the lines firmer – a complex process that sometimes entailed a series of eighty rough sketches. A far cry from the quintessential apparent simplicity. Furthermore, Gruau always kept control over page layout like an art director over his visuals.

Photography and its many derivatives that emerged after World War II probably finished off the art of large illustrations. It has now been reduced to a slightly offbeat anecdote of a few rare drawings printed in luxury magazines dealing with high fashion and perfume. After the semi-retirement and then death of Carl Erikson (Eric) in 1958, the artist René Bouché, his junior, remained the leading figure in illustration, working for *Vogue*, the most prestigious publication of its kind. Was it his sudden death in 1963 that led Condé Nast publications and its art director Alex Lieberman to completely drop graphic illustrations and use photos instead? With the emergence of ready-made clothing, a young, more spontaneous, and less couture-oriented style appeared. It favored young photographers and hip girls that bore virtually no relation to the pretty women wearing Dior or Balmain hats and gloves. Yet the astonishing longevity of René Gruau remains as he closes the loop of a cycle begun just one century earlier.

True, photography sees everything, but it does not explain much. Who will describe the rustling of a silhouette in a ballroom dress? Who will suspend time to the swirl of a fragrance? Who will offer this theater of illusion – fashion, adornment and luxury itself – characters as memorable as those sketched by the ever-steady hand of the son of an attractive woman and an Italian count? A whiplash signature with a star set above it: quite simply, Gruau.

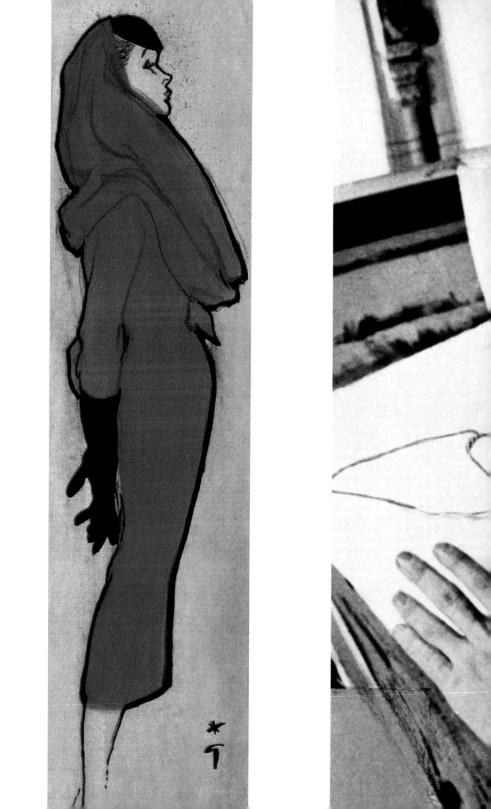

MOLYNEUX

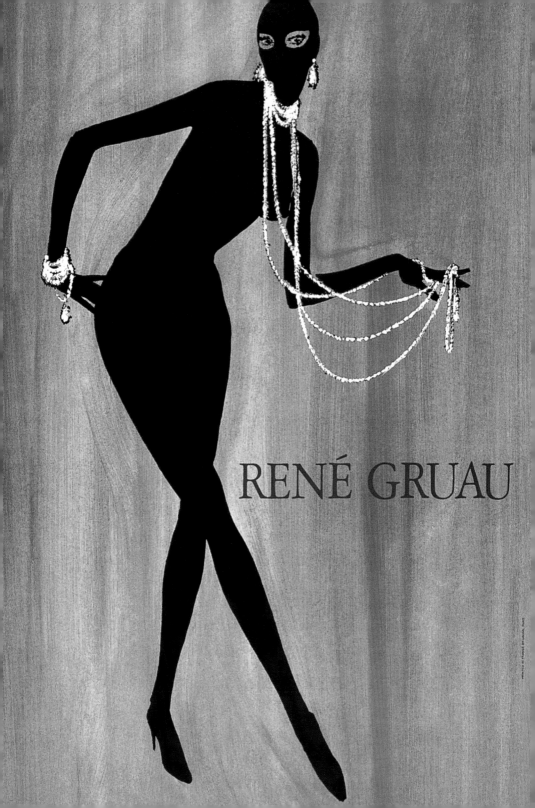

RENÉ GRUAU

Christian Dior

Souliers créés par

Roger Vivier

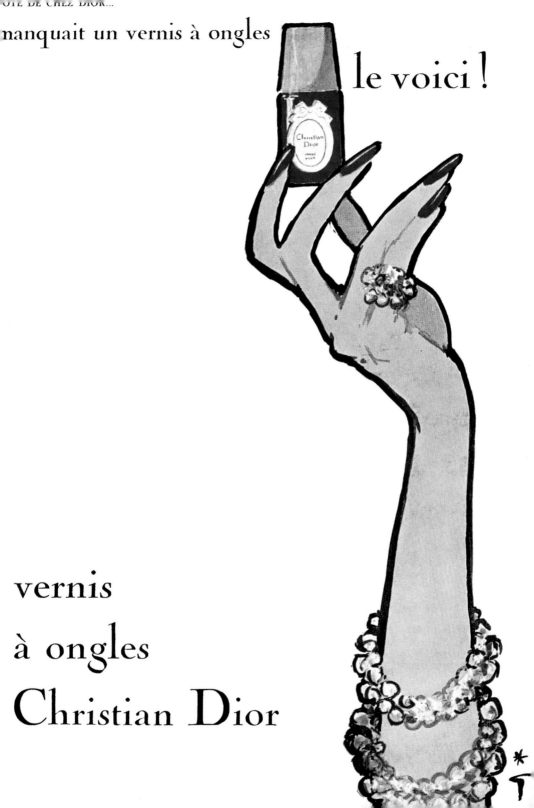

Elizabeth Arden

7, PLACE VENDÔME, PARIS · OPÉRA 42-4

JACQUES FATH

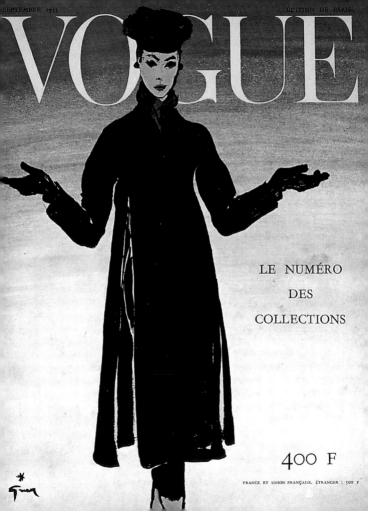

SEPTEMBRE 1955   ÉDITION DE PARIS

VOGUE

LE NUMÉRO

DES

COLLECTIONS

400 F

FRANCE ET UNION FRANÇAISE, ÉTRANGER : 500 F

Fourrures de Printemps

CHARME
ÉLÉGANCE

PARIS

COLLECTIONS
DE
PRINTEMPS

1964

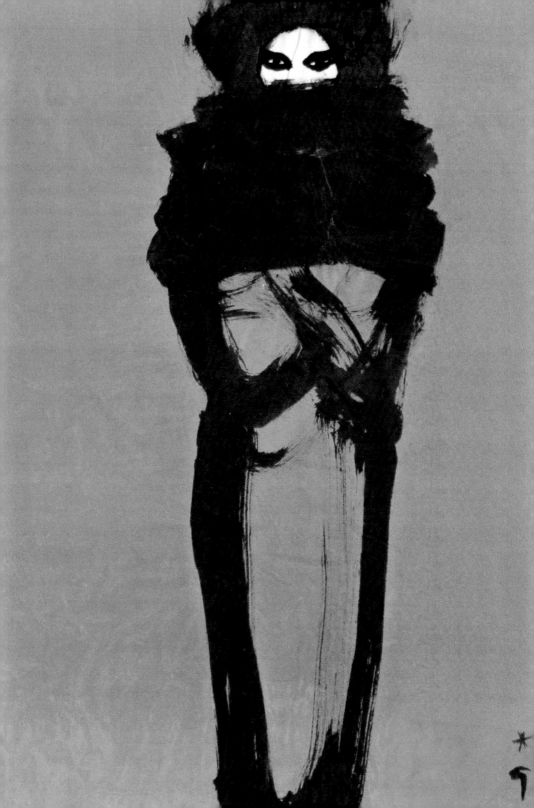

pour la haute mode..........

feutres

Montézin

Chronology

1909: Born Count Renato Zavagli-Ricciardelli delle Caminate, in Rimini, Italy, of an Italian father and French mother.
Begins to draw at a very early age, publishing his first drawings at the age of 14. At 18, he was already published in Italy, England and Germany.

1924: Moves to Paris with his mother and takes on her name: Gruau. Gives up the idea of becoming an architect and decides to be a fashion illustrator.

1935-1939: Begins his collaboration with *Fémina*, *Marie Claire*, *L'Officiel*, *Le Magazine du Figaro*, and with American and English publications.

1940: Seeks refuge in Lyon, where he draws for *Marie Claire*.

1946: First job for *International Textiles*, a magazine for which he was to draw every cover through 1984.

1947: Beginning of a great professional friendship with Christian Dior. Their two names were to remain intimately tied. Publication of the famous first advertisements for *Dior Parfum* and *Miss Dior*.

1948: Leaves for the United States to work with *Harper's Bazaar* and *Vogue*. Two years later, he becomes the exclusive artist for *Flair*.

1949: Draws the famous *Rouge Baiser* poster and does the cover for *Club* magazine.

1956-1963: Creates theater costumes and sets, and makes posters for the famous Parisian cabarets *Lido* and *Moulin Rouge*.

1964-1970: Mainly makes poster advertisements for Blizzard rain coats, Pellet socks, Peroche pants, and for Bemberg, Eminence and Pancaldi perfumery.

1980-1989: In parallel with advertising, Gruau returns to fashion illustrations with French *Vogue*, *Madame Figaro*, *Elle*, and *L'Officiel de la Couture* and *Ode* in 1955.

1989-1999: Continues to work with the leading names in high fashion (Dior, Givenchy, Omega, etc.) and for perfume and cosmetics companies.

2000-2001: Two permanent René Gruau exhibition rooms are opened in the museum of the city of Rimini, Italy.

Main exhibits

1977: Musée de la Mode et du Costume, palais Galliera, Paris: *Elégance et Créations. 1945-1975.*

1984: Musée de la Mode et du Costume, palais Galliera, Paris: *Modes et Lettre du XVIIIe siècle à nos jours.*

1985: Musée historique des Tissus de Lyon: *Hommage à Balenciaga.*
Musée de la Mode et du Costume, palais Galliera, Paris: *Pierre Balmain et 40 ans de création.*

1986: Musée de l'Affiche et de la Publicité, Paris: *Mode et Publicité, 1985-1986; Le "look" Marie Claire.*

1987: Musée des Arts de la Mode, Paris: *Hommage à Christian Dior, 1947-1957.*

1989: Musée de la Mode et du Costume, palais Galliera, Paris: *Gruau, Mode et Publicité.*

1990: Museum für Angegervandte Kunst, Cologne: *René Gruau, 40 years of illustrations and drawings.*

1991: Fashion Institute of Technology, New York: *René Gruau.*

1992: Villa Lamartine, Monaco: *René Gruau.*
The Space, Hanae Mori Building, Tokyo: *Fashion.*
Academia di Costume e di Moda, Rome: *René Gruau Interprete del moderno.*

1993: Piazza Cavour, Sala dell'Argengo, Rimini: *Un riminese a Parigi.*

1995: La Malmaison, Cannes: *Hommage à René Gruau.*

1998: Year of France in Japan Mitsukoshi/Homiuri Shimbun René Gruau *Master of Elegance* – Tokyo – Sapporo – Niigata – Nagoya - Fukuoka.

1999-2000: Opening of first advertisement museum with *Passionément René Gruau* – Union Centrale des Arts Décoratifs – Palais du Louvre, Paris.

In addition to these major exhibits, the Galeries Sylvie Nissen presented *René Gruau from 1994 to today* in Hong Kong, Singapore and Thailand.

From end June to end August 2002, Sylvie Nissen organized a fashion exhibit, *René Gruau Retrospective*, at the Palazzo Pitti, Florence.

For more information, visit:
- the artist's site: www.rene-gruau.com <http://www.rene-gruau.com>
- the link to the Musée des Arts Décoratifs: www.ucad.fr <http://www.ucad.fr>

Créée
pour
la
ligne
Dior

la gaine
Christian Dior

GAINES ET GORGES

Gruau

Illustration for *L'Officiel* (1950). © All rights reserved.
René Gruau in his Paris apartment. He is 40 years old.
© Galerie Bartsch & Chariau.

Bettina for the first Givenchy collection. © Chevallier.
Bettina in the same period. © Galerie Bartsch & Chariau.

Illustration for Moyneux, for the magazine *Silhouette* (1950).
© Archives Sylvie Nissen.

Advertisement for Christian Dior stockings (1953). © Private collection.
Illustration for Jantzen USA (1950). © Galerie Sylvie Nissen.

Advertisement for Jacques Fath jewelry (1950). © Galerie Bartsch & Chariau.

Boussac raincoat for Blizzand (1965). © Laurent Sully-Jaulmes.
Illustration for Jacques Fath, for *L'Officiel* (1949). © Galerie Bartsch & Chariau.

Advertisement for Ortalion stockings, for Bemberg. © Galerie Bartsch & Chariau.
Advertisement for *Rouge Baiser* lipstick (1949). © Private collection.

Advertisements for Christian Dior. © Archives Sylvie Nissen.

Advertisement for Christian Dior stockings. © Galerie Bartsch & Chariau.
Lucien Lelong evening dress (Spring/Summer 1946). © Private collection.

Cover for *International Textiles* (1960). © Archives Sylvie Nissen.
Cover for *International Textiles* (1950). © Archives Sylvie Nissen.

Cover for *International Textiles* (1946). © Archives Sylvie Nissen.
Pierre Balmain dress for *L'Officiel* (1953). © Laurent Sully-Jaulmes.

Illustration for the magazine *Silhouette* (1948). © Galerie Bartsch & Chariau.

Advertisement for Elizabeth Arden lipstick (1945).
© Archives Sylvie Nissen.
Illustration for Jacques Fath (1947-1948). © Galerie Bartsch & Chariau.

Pierre Balmain dress (1952). © Galerie Bartsch & Chariau.
Pierre Balmain dress for the magazine *Fémina* (1946).
© Galerie Bartsch & Chariau.

"Ispahan" evening gown by Christian Dior (1947). © Laurent Sully-Jaulmes.
Cover for *International Textiles* (1955). © Archives Sylvie Nissen.

Jacques Fath model (1950). © Galerie Bartsch & Chariau.

Cover for *Vogue* magazine. © Archives Sylvie Nissen.
Christian Dior dress for *L'Officiel*. © Archives Sylvie Nissen.

Pierre Balmain dress for *L'Officiel* (1953). © Galerie Bartsch & Chariau.
Advertisement for "spring furs" (1950). © Laurent Sully-Jaulmes.

Red Sofa (1988). © Archives Sylvie Nissen.

Cover for *International Textiles* (1964). © Archives Sylvie Nissen.
Cover for *International Textiles* (1970s). © Archives Sylvie Nissen.

Illustration of hat and muff designed by Paulette (1952). © All rights reserved.

Robert Piguet dresses for *L'Officiel* (1955). © Galerie Bartsch & Chariau.

Illustration for Pierre Balmain published in *L'Officiel*. © Private collection.
"Gruau" evening gown designed by Christian Dior (1949-1950). © Private collection.

Givenchy dress for *L'Officiel* (1953). © Laurent Sully-Jaulmes.
Cover for *International Textiles* (1955). © Archives Sylvie Nissen.

Illustration of a Givenchy dress – first collection (1952). © Private collection.
René Gruau and Bettina during a work session (1950). © D.R.

Study (1960). © Galerie Bartsch & Chariau.
Illustration for *Club Magazine* (1960). © Private collection.

Robert Piguet dresses for *Fémina* (1957). © All rights reserved.
René Gruau in his Paris home, drawing a Pierre Balmain dress (1995).
© Thierre Chomel/*Vogue*.

Montézin felt hat (1955). © Archives Sylvie Nissen.
René Gruau in his Cannes home (1989). © Archives Sylvie Nissen.

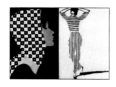

Cover for *International Textiles* (1960). © Archives Sylvie Nissen.
Cover for *International Textiles* (1954). © Archives Sylvie Nissen.

The publisher wishes to thank René Gruau, Sylvie Nissen and Yann de Saint-Sulpice for their help in preparing this book.

Also, thanks to Bettina, Laurent Sully-Jaulmes et Thierry Chomel.

Lastly, this book could not have been made without the helpful contributions of the Galerie Sylvie Nissen (Carlton, Cannes), Joëlle Chariau (Galerie Bartsch & Chariau, Munich), Sylviane (*Elle*/Scoop) and *Vogue*.

I extend my thanks to them.